Envy, Anger & Sweet Revenge

HEY, IT WORKS IN HOLLYWOOD!

SIN SERIES

VOLUME V

Envy, Anger & Sweet Revenge

HEY, IT WORKS IN HOLLYWOOD!

STEPHEN M. SILVERMAN

RED ROCK PRESS, NEW YORK

PRINTED IN HONG KONG

TABLE OF CONTENTS

*This book is dedicated
to Judith Crist,
ever-temperate and ever-loving,
most of the time.*

INTRODUCTION
IN THE TIME OF CHOLER

I should not be writing this book. I am not angry. I am not envious. I do not seek revenge. I don't even seek another writing credit. I certainly don't need to be sitting at this keyboard all day, especially when it is so nice outside. I could be at the beach instead, lying in the sun. But I am a redhead. I have fair skin. I can't lie in the sun. I wish I had darker skin. I wish I were taller. I wish I were Michael Jordan. Then I could kick sand in everybody's face at the beach. I'd be rich, too, and could tell the "Sin Series" publishers to just go screw. If they had something better to do, then I wouldn't be stuck with this stupid task of finding things to say about envy, anger and sweet revenge.

Oh, sure, I know what you're thinking: You're a redhead, and all redheads have hot tempers. But who the hell are you to say that? You're just jealous because your name isn't on the cover of this book. But your envy will get you nowhere—not that I expect writing this will bring me much, either. Frankly, I'd rather that my name be on a royalty check addressed to Stephen King.

Of course, I'm only pulling your leg. Staring sin in the face always does that to me.

Now, on to the serious part of our program: the sins at hand, envy and anger or, as I like to call them, Mary and Bob. Envy often leads to anger, but envy is not necessarily the root of all anger. Freud would tell us that our parents are. Well, I had very loving parents. My mother loved Cary Grant, and my father loved Carmel, California. What they thought of me I'll never know, because ours was not an expressive family. (My parents are now deceased, which does anger me.) My mother used to say, however, that people shouldn't be called *mad*. Dogs are mad, as in the Noel Coward song, "Mad Dogs and Englishmen." People, she would say, are *angry*.

As I grew older, I learned that even my mother could be wrong. People get mad. How else to explain Eminem?

In the 1976 movie *Network*, written by Paddy Chayefsky (whose gifts of perception I envy), the slightly—and then, gradually, very—mad (as in nuts) newscaster Howard Beale, masterfully played by Peter Finch, howls at his viewing public, "I'm mad as hell, and I'm not going to take it anymore."

His bray entered the popular consciousness and became something of a rallying cry, which was odd, because in 1976 there didn't seem to be that much to get hopped up about. Nixon was already gone, and Kathie Lee Gifford was still nowhere on the horizon. Still, it was the Establishment, also known as the System, that irked our hero. Beale's ultimate revenge on the unseen but nonetheless potent forces that were driving him to the brink was to blow his own brains out on national television during prime time, which, of course, is what inspired *Survivor*.

But enough of poor Howard. What about me? Specifically, *why me*? Why has the System, or, in this case, the publishers of this book, summoned me for the task at hand? I am not a philosopher. I am not a cleric. I am not a behavioral specialist. But I do live in New York, which come to think of it, has been described as the angriest and most envious city in the world. New

Angry or Mad? Howard Beale (PETER FINCH), the incendiary prophet of *Network*, is both, which makes him a mascot for red-hot Hollywood.

MGM/United Artists, 1976

York, I've been told, is where "F – you!" was invented. Not that I necessarily find this atmosphere of contention to exist. Given the population density here, most of us have been forced to adopt some, if not numerous, social graces—certainly more than are practiced in my birthplace, Los Angeles, where Road Rage appears to be as rampant as gang warfare, smog and rolling black-outs. So perhaps I am a behavioral specialist, after all.

But I would like to think that I was asked to write this book, which I will get to in a minute (an introduction was not even part of my contract), because I also happened to have written the biography of Stanley Donen, the man who directed the movie *Bedazzled,* no, not the tepid, Lipton-tea 2000 version with Elizabeth Hurley and Brendan Fraser, but the strong, 1968 original *cuppa* with Peter Cook and Dudley Moore. Cook is George Spiggot, aka the Devil; Moore is his would-be disciple, a short-order cook named Stanley Moon. In supporting roles, actor Robert Russell plays the embodiment of rage—a character called Anger; and Barry Humphries, later to become known as the great Dame Edna, is Envy. (Raquel Welch delivers a revealing cameo as Lust, but—wouldn't you know it?—that wasn't the sin to which I was assigned.) All seven lively deadlies are in the employ of Spiggot/Beelzebub. ("Rotten sins I've got working for me," he moans. "Must be the wages.")

And while Stanley Moon has exchanged his miserable soul for the assurance of true love and good fortune, the poor slob's search ends up going all to hell as he encounters each sin. Envy presents himself as a bitchy old queen; Anger materializes as the brawny bouncer at Spiggot's headquarters, a nightclub that Stanley describes as being decorated "in early Hitler." Neither Envy nor Anger is anyone Stanley wishes to spend any time with. How well I can see his point.

Although I am not a conscious devotee of Envy and Anger, I am no stranger to Revenge fantasies. (I refer to revenge, by the way, as Norman.) There was once this Hollywood producer who strung me along for months on a project. I so wanted her large derriere to split her skirt wide open as she climbed into her red Mercedes convertible in front of the Beverly Wilshire. Then there was this avaricious publisher for whom I once worked. I simply wanted him to misplace a ten-dollar bill, for I knew that alone would kill him.

As it is, I am content to remain an observer and allow jealousy and rage to unfold before me as fictional elements on stage and screen. For without the potent, primal forces of envy and anger, drama—if not life itself—would feel as vapid as an episode of *Friends.* (I can sense the number of admirers I made with that last statement, and let me say I envy your lack of discrimination.)

As I plunge headfirst into this anecdotal exploration of sin, I must confess to bringing to this book a set of generational biases. These are not hateful, because hate connotes not only anger but also ignorance, and I hate ignorant people. I particularly hate prejudiced people. But beyond that, I love everybody, except lawyers. I am a Baby Boomer; this I cannot deny, so some of the references contained herein may reflect that narrowness of view.

With that in mind, it is time to focus on business. And so I'd sincerely like to thank the publishers, Ilene and Richard Barth of Red Rock Press, and apologize for my earlier rant in which I suggested that they just go screw. Everybody knows that married people don't do that, anyway. And I'd like to thank my pal, Evelyn Renold, for the loan of the book, *Dear Sir, Drop Dead!*, and for having introduced me to the Barths in the first place, all those many years ago. And thanks to Jim Martin for introducing me to Evelyn, even longer ago. To Barbara Grizzuti Harrison, I say thanks for explaining the Bible to me. Ditto to Chris Hill for topping my jokes. And thanks to Nina Pinsky, just for the heck of it.

The friendship among us all is enviable.

—STEPHEN M. SILVERMAN

CHAPTER ONE

CURTAIN

UP

Jealousy entered English via the French masculine *jaloux* and feminine *jalousie*. *Jalousie* is also a chic name for the Venetian blind, open or closed—to keep out prying eyes. The word dallied in Latin but it was first the Greek word, *zelous*, meaning fervor, warmth, ardor or intense desire.

Surely the link between curtain and jealous is not accidental, although envy is so primal that it must have existed long before some Italian designer stole the concept for his modern window treatment.

There are, after all, no Venetian blinds in the Bible. But there one will find ample cases of envy (as well as anger and revenge).

Zeus only knows if there were any Venetian blinds on Mount Olympus, but nary an illustrator showed them hanging from the Parthenon. Even so, many an Olympian-inspired drama tells of titanic-sized jealousy, followed by, in supporting roles, wrath and revenge.

Genesis: the Back Story

Actual notes from a pitch meeting for a film based on *Paradise Lost* by John Milton (1608-1674).

"OK, think *Spy Kids*, only naked, meet a bunch of evil *Charlie's Angels*. A bouncer named Stan (Sean Hayes of *Will & Grace* in his first film stretch), is sitting around the Hellfire club, furious, because nothing is going on. He's been sentenced there since losing his spot at the rival, Heaven, which is where all the current action is. Envious, he seduces some other club-goers into backing his effort to reclaim his former position.

"One of them, Bob (Chris Rock), proposes bypassing Heaven altogether and taking over some new club, Eden. Stan proposes that he try to crash the place himself.

"Stan gets directions to Eden from a cappo, Oriel (David Arquette). The big boss at Eden, Al Mighty (Russell Crowe), gets word of Stan's impending arrival, and tips off his two favorite patrons, Harvard MBAs Adam (Justin Timberlake) and Eve (Britney Spears), as to just how dangerous this guy is. Typically, Eve doesn't pay attention, but Adam does.

"On first inspection, Stan is consumed by jealously over the beauty of Eden. His only way to wreak revenge: Destroy it. He spies on Adam and Eve, who are getting ready for Reptile Night at the club. They're going as cute chameleons. Stan goes as a snake. He begins his wave of destruction by telling Eve that her costume makes her look fat. Soldiers working for Al try to stop Stan, but the slithery villain escapes.

"Eventually, Stan succeeds in getting Eve alone, and offers her a job at the Hellfire Club. They seal their

Back When It Was Fun: *Adam and Eve* by Erté

Eve in her chameleon costume for "Reptile Night" at the Eden Club; trouble began when the snake told Eve she looked fat.

budding business deal with a green apple martini, and Eve comes home drunk and tells Adam of her plan. Furious, but not wanting to lose Eve, he too has a green apple martini. Next thing you know, both of them are alcoholics.

"Al is seething, because *Vogue* was going to do a big photo shoot of Adam and Eve at Eden. A gang war breaks out, and Adam and Eve, feeling remorseful for having started it, tell Al that they'll do anything to receive his forgiveness. Stan, meanwhile, claims a premature victory and heads back to the Hellfire Club with the good news. Al, meanwhile, assigns his second in command, the accountant, Michael (John Travolta), to get Adam and Eve into a 12-step program. They are also told they can never return to Eden.

"Rather than celebrate Stan's accomplishment, his cronies come at him with forked tongues. They call him 'wimp' and other things.

"Meanwhile, the IRS shuts Eden down for back taxes. And Adam and Eve ride off into the sunset in an SUV, with a personalized license plate reading 'Noah's Ark.' Adam is swigging from a bottle, but Eve—who looks knocked-up—is off the juice."

Studio Coverage
"Weak story. No legs. Also may be problems with Milton estate (very Puritanical). On plus side: kiddie-market spin-off possibilities with snake and chameleon costumes (not exploited by Woody with *Zelig*); primo premiere party prospects. Is DiCaprio still looking for a comeback vehicle?"

Green Apple Martini

1 ounce apple schnapps
1 ounce vodka
1 ounce apple juice

In a cocktail shaker filled with ice, combine the above. Shake or stir with malicious intent. Pour into martini glasses and garnish with a thin slice of Granny Smith apple.

Family Matters: The Early Years Meet the Cast!

CAIN: First couple's first born. Cain was a tiller of the ground, but only mediocre at it. Otherwise, he'd have owned the entire garden and subdivided.

ABEL: A very successful keeper of sheep, a fact that antagonizes his older, underachieving brother.

> Now have you read of the fable of Cain and Abel?
> Once they were in a scandal that shook the town.
> Cain became mighty jealous of brother Abel,
> So he rose up and smote Abel down.
> Now the Lord sure was hopping mad,
> And yet he was plenty sad,
> To think that he had a man like Cain.
>
> The Lord spoke and showed his wrath,
> And Cain walked the path
> That led to a life full of pain.
>
> You can't run from the shadow of retribution.
> If you're bad then you gotta pay for your wrongs.
> Let yourself take a lesson from Cain and Abel:
>
> Don't lament, be content,
> Don't resent what the Lord has sent,
> And you'll find that you're bound to get along.
> —LOUIS ARMSTRONG, *The Gospel According to Louis*

Back When It Wasn't Fun: *The Murder of Abel*, by A. Sacchi

KIMBER & SHARTLESS *QUARTO BIBLE,* STEREOTYPE EDITION

WARDROBE ENVY: A SEMINAL CASE

Before Liberace, before Elton John, there lived in the land of Canaan a lad named Joseph, who would come to have a "coat of many colors" (Genesis 37:3). Joseph was the son of Rachel and Jacob, who had eleven other boys, though Joseph was clearly Jacob's favorite—as good a shepherd as any father could desire, and kind and loving to boot. It's no wonder Donny Osmond toured as Joseph in the Andrew Lloyd Webber/Tim Rice musical.

However, the way Jacob doted on his second youngest fueled the envy inside Joseph's brothers, and this jealousy was only exacerbated once Jacob gave Joseph a dazzling, bespoke coat. His brothers, meanwhile, were stuck with buying off the rack, retail.

Compounded with the problem of the gift was also the fact that Joseph was something of a dreamer, whose tireless intuition told him that one day he would become a great man and far more successful than his siblings. Actually, it's a wonder Barbra Streisand didn't play him in the musical.

Irritated by Joseph's lack of humility, his brothers attacked him in the field, stripped him of his coat and were about to toss him into a pit to face certain death when, suddenly, a roving band of Ishmaelites happened to pass by. Ishmaelites did that in those days.

Seizing upon a business opportunity, the brothers sold Joseph as a slave and returned to their father and informed him that Joseph had died.

But the story doesn't die there. Through strength of character and his belief in God, Joseph overcame all obstacles and became the Governor of Egypt, a more profitable occupation than shepherd. In time, Joseph saved his family from the famine that overtook the land and was reunited with his beloved father. He never did get back the coat, however.

Pretty Woman Meets the Godfather

The Philistines, the original Mob, envied the Children of Israel (someone always does). They particularly envied Samson's strength. So they made the beautiful Delilah an offer she couldn't refuse and dispatched her to find out the secret of Samson's power, a portion of which she, er, sampled every night.

It wasn't merely Samson's physical strength that made the Philistines green with envy, but his spiritual strength. Samson was reared under a Nazarite vow, meaning that he was never to cut his hair, never to drink wine and never to touch a dead body. (The last one was a snap.) He was to live his whole life dedicated to the will of God.

Not that anybody's perfect. Samson's one weakness was his love of pretty women. Nightly, the gorgeous Delilah (think Hedy Lamarr) would suggest to Samson that if he truly loved her, he would share the secret of his strength. Despite her repeated inquiries, and the fact that he would awake to find himself tied up with seven bowstrings and the like, Samson didn't seem terribly aware that Delilah might have had ulterior motives.

Nevertheless, Delilah wanted the money that the Philistine Mob had promised her for revealing Samson's secret, so she cried to her lover, accusing him of not really loving her. Finally, Samson caved in. He admitted that his strength came from his hair.

That night, Delilah arranged for her lover to get a clip job, and there went his strength. The Philistines took him as their slave, and Delilah got her money and a terrible reputation.

That, at least, was one version. Samson had a lot of script problems and therefore a lot of screenwriters (a lot like *Tootsie* and *Town & Country*). In a previous telling, Samson had a wife who was approached by the Mob with a promise not to burn down her father's house if she could help them out a little.

Still, there's always a big finish, with the Philistines being crushed thanks to a revengeful (but God-forgiven) Samson.

The first "Pretty Woman," Delilah (HEDY LAMARR), secretly trained as a hair-dresser.

A Sister Thing in Hollywood

In their heydays, Olivia de Havilland (born 1916) and her sister, Joan Fontaine (born 1917) were as well-known for their ongoing rivalry as they were for their Oscar-winning roles.

In 1987, Fontaine elaborated on this theme to interviewer Gregory Speck: "Let me put it like this: I just got a golden retriever puppy for my one-year-old German shepherd, who was looking to me for too much love and attention. At the pet shop, the first thing they said was that I must break it very gently to the older dog, so that his nose did not get out of joint when he saw the intruder. They told me that he would be jealous and that I should give him more love than before.

"Well, apparently no one said that to my parents. My sister's nose got out of joint immediately and never got set straight. My mother told me that Olivia would not even look into the crib after I arrived. She has always felt I was an intruder.

"Look at what happened in our careers: I got the Oscar first, got married first, had the first child . . . usurping her position all the time.

"I talked to a child psychologist who wanted to write a book about us, and he said that it's gone on too long to be undone. Through no fault of my own, everything I did upstaged her, for I'm an achiever. Up against an achiever and a usurper, an older sister doesn't stand a chance."

Not that de Havilland didn't accomplish a few things, too. As Fontaine conceded, "She was up for the Oscar for *Gone With the Wind*, *Hold Back the Dawn* and *The Snake Pit*, and I think she won twice, for *To Each His Own* and *The Heiress*.

"Anyway, our feud would never have become so legendary if the magazines had not picked up on it and blown it all out of proportion. Olivia's a berater, and she loved to tell me off. I guess that's when I learned to walk away, which enraged her even more."

Not to be outdone, de Havilland offered her view of sisterly devotion to the press in 1999. Asked if she and Joan might ever reconcile, she replied "Out of the question."

This page: Olivia de Havilland
Left: Joan Fontaine

The Envy-lope, Please

The first Oscars—actually called the Homers—were held in the original Shrine Auditorium, on Mt. Olympus, to celebrate achievement in the lives of the Greek Gods. In the truest definition of the term "performers," these founding fathers and mothers personified envy, anger and revenge in their daily deeds. Dramatists have relied on their role models ever since.

Token trophies were also dealt to "Mere Mortals," the precursor of the scientific and technical category awards. The host for this original event was Zeus, which in ancient Greek means Billy Crystal. And the Homers went to:

Best Goddess in a Leading Jealous Role

APHRODITE, for envying the virginity of Hestia. Accepting the award for Aphrodite was her son Phobos (Fear), although he was afraid to tell the audience that his mother was busy with a new production in Cythera, so his sibling, Demos (Terror) got up and scared the hell out of the crowd.

Best Goddess in a Supporting Jealous Role

ARTEMIS, who, for starters, told her father Zeus to give her as many names as her brother Apollo. Dad complied, as he was aware of her short temper. Scene shown on Homer night: That of the young Actaeon, who chances upon the goddess as she's bathing on Mt. Cithaeron. Enraged, Artemis changes him into a stag, whereupon he is pursued and killed by his own hounds. Standing ovation. (Or else.)

Best Mere Mortal in an Angry Role (Leading or Supporting)

ELECTRA, who, after her mother, Clytemnestra, and Aegisthus murdered her father, Agamemnon, sought revenge and longed for the return of her brother, Orestes. According to Euripides (best screenwriter winner), Electra also took an active role in the killing of her mother, which may have tipped the scales for her winning her award.

Best Performance by a Barbarian Witch

MEDEA, who, having betrayed her family to help her lover Jason win the Golden Fleece, then found him courting another woman, the daughter of King Creon of Corinth. After failing to persuade Jason to return to her, Medea decided to kill her rival with a gift of poisoned clothing. She also opted to kill her children. "I know indeed what evil I intend to do," she declaimed, "but stronger than all my afterthoughts is my fury—fury that brings upon mortals the greatest evils." Medea's appearance at the Homers was made through special arrangement with King Aegeus of Athens.

Best Special Effects

ATHENA, for her major makeover of Medusa. Medusa's beauty was such that the envious Athena transformed her rival's hair into live snakes and set a curse upon her, so that when someone looked at Medusa he would be turned into stone. Said to be the inspiration for Ethan Hawke's acting.

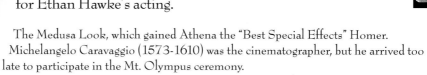

The Medusa Look, which gained Athena the "Best Special Effects" Homer. Michelangelo Caravaggio (1573-1610) was the cinematographer, but he arrived too late to participate in the Mt. Olympus ceremony.

Top prize, Best God in a Leading Role

ZEUS, because who could argue with the landlord? He also tosses a mean thunderbolt. Because he was in the bathroom at the time of the announcement, however, Zeus' award was accepted by Briareus, a giant with fifty heads and a hundred hands. Unfortunately, he helped himself to all the remaining Homers, too.

Overheard At the Acropolis

"Envy slays itself by its own arrows."
—ANONYMOUS CITIZEN

"Anger is a short madness."
—HOMER

"It is in the nature of very few men to honor without envy a friend who has prospered." —AESCHYLUS

Find the Envy Here

"To men of judgment and honor he is intolerable, his arrogance is insufferable, and all honest men detest his malice." —PLUTARCH ON ARISTOPHANES

"The only genius with an IQ of 60."
—GORE VIDAL ON ANDY WARHOL

"He's a two-bit, pretentious academic and he can't play rock 'n' roll, because he's a loser."
—LOU REED ON FRANK ZAPPA

"He bores me. He ought to have stuck to his flying machines."
—AUGUSTE RENOIR ON LEONARDO DA VINCI

"[Her] career is a testimony to menopausal chic."
—ERICA JONG ON JOAN COLLINS

"A slur upon the moral government of the world."
—JOHN QUINCY ADAMS ON THOMAS JEFFERSON

Subject to Jongian analysis, Joan Collins

"A glorified bandmaster!" —SIR THOMAS BEECHAM ON ARTURO TOSCANINI

"One of the nicest old ladies I ever met." —WILLIAM FAULKNER ON HENRY JAMES

"A combination of Little Nell and Lady Macbeth." —ALEXANDER WOOLLCOTT ON DOROTHY PARKER

"A truck driver in drag." —TRUMAN CAPOTE ON JACQUELINE SUSANN

"She has more chins than the Hong Kong phone book." —JOAN RIVERS ON ELIZABETH TAYLOR

"Ronald Reagan doesn't dye his hair, he's just prematurely orange." —GERALD FORD

"Not merely awful . . . I would consider it sacrilegious to say anything less than that they are godawful."
—WILLIAM F. BUCKLEY ON THE BEATLES

"The enviably attractive nephew who sings an Irish ballad for the company and then winsomely disappears before the table-clearing and dishwashing begin."
—LYNDON B. JOHNSON ON JOHN F. KENNEDY

FULLY RESTORED TO ORSON WELLES' ORIGINAL VISION!

CHARLTON **HESTON**

JANET **LEIGH**

ORSON **WELLES**

in

TOUCH OF EVIL

SCREENPLAY BY **ORSON WELLES** • PRODUCED BY **ALBERT ZUGSMITH**
DIRECTED BY **ORSON WELLES**

"There, but for the grace of God, goes God."
—HERMAN MANCKIEWICZ ON ORSON WELLES

A Pop Quiz

Free cable. Free the hostages. *Free Willy*. Only one is enviable. Name it.

Wardrobe Envy Update

Model-turned-movie-star-in-the-making, Chloe Sevigny measuring her, uh, peers for *Harper's Bazaar*:

NICOLE KIDMAN – "[Christian Dior paid her] like a million dollars to wear those dresses!"

KATE HUDSON – "People are saying [she] is fashionable now; boring to me."

CHARLIZE THERON – "Tacky."

From the Temple Times

"Wrath is cruel and anger is outrageous, but who is able to stand before envy?"
—*Proverbs*, 27:4

"Envy and wrath shorten the life, and carefulness bringeth age before the time."
—*Apocrypha* (Ecclesiasticus, 30:24)

From Our Far-Flung Correspondents

"Pride, Envy and Avarice are the three sparks that have set these hearts on fire." —Alighieri Dante, *The Divine Comedy*

"From pride, vainglory and hypocrisy; from envy, hatred and malice and all uncharitableness, Good Lord deliver us." —*The Book of Common Prayer*

What's Playing in Cleveland?

Midwesterners, unlike denizens of Hollywood, are known for their straight talk. Witness their answers to the inquiry posed by the aptly-named *Cleveland Plain Dealer*: "Did you outgrow your sibling rivalry?"

"Yes, I outgrew it many years ago, but my dumb brother and sister have not. They are such babies."

"My sister and I are in our 40s, and we outgrew our sibling rivalry years ago. Now if my younger sister would just stop blaming me for not being a ballerina, and if people would stop confusing me with my older sister, I would be fine."

"Heck, no. I'm 43 years old, and my sister still thinks she's boss."

"I didn't know that we had any sibling rivalry among my three brothers and two sisters until my mother had to sell the house and move into a high-rise because of congestive heart failure. And, all of a sudden, everyone's coming over and getting her stuff appraised. Then there was a lot of sibling rivalry. It's at such a point now, I think we can go on 'Oprah.'"

"I think we were like millions of others: we never had sibling rivalries. We had sibling cheerleading for each other."

"Yes, thankfully, I did outgrow my sibling rivalry, but my fat, stupid, money-grubbing sister never did. My brothers are much better."

"I never had sibling rivalry, but my sisters and one brother still hate my guts to this day."

Mamie
Eisenhower
appraising
Jackie Kennedy

ROBERT KNUDSEN, JUNE 22, 1962, WHITE HOUSE/JOHN F. KENNEDY LIBRARY

Overheard At the Rialto

"Envy is a pain of mind that successful men cause their neighbors."
—ONASANDER

"It is better to be envied than pitied."
—HERODOTUS

CHAPTER TWO

No Biz Like

Envy Biz

G reen grow the lilacs . . . and the palm trees . . . and the entertainment industry. This has gone on for some time. In the 17th century, Molière, who was both an actor and a playwright, observed, "The envious will die, but envy never."

He wasn't kidding.

Nouveau riche Gatsby (ROBERT REDFORD) envied it all: the houses, the gardens, the careless confidence of the well-born—all summed up in Daisy (MIA FARROW).

Gorillas In Our Midst

The Great Envy Novel:
The Great Gatsby by F. Scott Fitzgerald

The Great Envy Movie:
Billy Wilder's *Love in the Afternoon*

The Great Envy Television Program:
Who Wants to Be a Millionaire?

MOZART'S MONKEY

Men say there is no justice on the earth
But neither is there justice in heaven.
By vigorous and tense persistence,
At last, within the boundless realm of music
I reached a lofty place. At last fame deigned
To smile on me; and in the hearts of men
I found an echo to my own creation.
Then I was happy, and enjoyed in peace
My labors, my success, my fame—nor less
The labors and successes of my friends,
My fellow-workers in the art divine.
No! Never did I know the sting of envy,
Oh, never! Neither when Piccinni* triumphed
In capturing the ears of skittish Paris,
Nor the first time there broke upon my sense
Iphigenia's opening harmonies.
Who dares to say that even proud Salieri
Could stoop to envy, like a loathsome snake
Trampled upon by men, yet still alive
And impotently gnawing sand and dust?

*No one! . . . But now—myself I say it—now
I do know envy! Yes, Salieri envies,
Deeply, in anguish envies. O ye Heavens!
Where, where is justice, when the sacred gift,
When deathless genius comes not to reward
Perfervid love and utter self-denial,
And toils and strivings and beseeching prayers,
But puts her halo round a lack-wit's skull,
A frivolous idler's brow? O Mozart, Mozart!*
—ALEXANDER PUSHKIN, *Mozart and Salieri*

Program Notes:

The voice-over narrator of this poem was originally one Johannes Chrysostomus Wolfgangus Theophilus Mozart (1756-91), an Austrian composer known on his record albums as Wolfgang Amadeus Mozart; "Wolfie" to his friends. Mozart died too young and too miserable to see himself in playwright Peter Shaffer's *Amadeus* on the West End or on Broadway played by Tim Curry (born 1946) or in the film version of the same, where he was impersonated by Thomas Hulce (born 1953).

SALIERI was originally played by Antonio Salieri (1750-1825), court composer to Emperor Joseph II, who was the brother of Marie Antoinette and a lover, in a limited sense, of music. Salieri was a man of all ambition and no genius, a potent combination that has long succeeded in the creative marketplace. Tony's posthumous stage and screen appearances were handled respectively by Ian McKellan (born 1939) and F. Murray Abraham (also born 1939), the former of whom won a 1981 Tony for his performance, and the latter, a 1984 Oscar, which of course speaks volumes about New York and Hollywood's admiration for the character.

ALEXANDER PUSHKIN (1799-1837), who also died young, was awarded no screen credit for his contribution, despite Hollywood's predilection for dead poets.

*NICCOLÒ PICCINNI (1728-1800) was an Italian opera composer whose fame was chiefly in France, albeit at a time when the French usually failed to recognize the achievements of anyone but the French. Talk about envy.

Antonio Salieri (F. MURRAY ABRAHAM) has been a jealousy pacesetter for 250 years but his rep became especially enviable after Peter Shaffer restored his seething, conniving prominence on stage and screen in *Amadeus*.

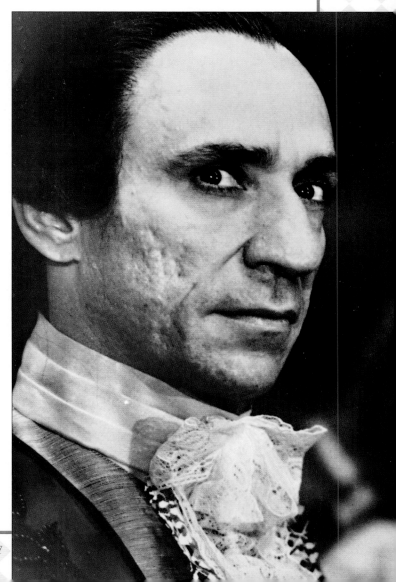

HANDKERCHIEF FOLLIES

Which of the following did Iago *not* say in *Othello*?

A) "His soul is so enfettered to her love
   That she may make, unmake, do what she
      list,
   Even as her appetite shall play the god
   With his weak function."

B) "For whiles this honest fool
   Plies Desdemona to repair his fortunes,
   And she for him pleads strongly to the Moor,
   So will I turn her virtue into pitch,
   And out of her own goodness make the net
   That shall enmesh them all."

C) "Love means never having to say you're
   sorry."

Mr. Edwin Forrest as Othello.

Why, why is this?
Think'st thou I make a life of jealousy,
To follow, still, the changes of the moon
With fresh suspicions?
—*Othello*, ACT III, SC. 3

38

Don't Shoot the Piano Player

Despite the legend and the Irving Berlin show, *Annie Get Your Gun*, sharpshooters Annie Oakley (1860-1926) and Frank Butler (1850-1926) were not rivals. In fact, they were very much in love and married. But you can't build a musical around that.

Theatrical Statements

"There is not a passion so strongly rooted in the human heart as envy."
—Richard Brinsley Sheridan, *The Critic*

"Envy's a coal comes hissing hot from hell."
—Philip James Bailey, *A Country Town*

"I'd rather have written *Cheers* than anything I've written."
—Kurt Vonnegut

MIDNIGHT IN THE GARDEN OF ELIZABETH ARDEN

Envy is the mortar that binds together the often-blockheaded characters in director George Cukor's 1939 film for MGM, *The Women*. Reviled by feminists, revered by gay men, the all-star film, based on Clare Boothe Luce's earlier and less-coherent play, is nothing more than a rapid-fire bitch-a-thon.

Her entire circle envies the wealthy and happily married Mary Haines (played by the weepy and cross-eyed Norma Shearer), and delights when they learn that her husband has strayed. He is the unseen Stephen. (Except in reference, no men appear in the movie, except for perhaps the man-ish Marjorie Main, as the owner of a Reno dude ranch where, ultimately, all the women wind up to await their divorces.)

One of the story's running gags is that the women learn the news about "poor Mary" from their mutual manicurist, a shrewish mouse who's been pushing the color Jungle Red. The shade becomes something of a catchphrase and a rallying cry.

Chief among the nags who are put out to pasture (Boothe is not complimentary toward her sisters) is Sylvia Fowler, played without an ounce of sympathy by Rosalind Russell. Her driving force is getting the goods on Mary. (In a 2001 Broadway revival, that role went to the Amazonian Kirsten Johnson, late of the sitcom *Third Rock from the Sun*. Cynthia Nixon, of *Sex and the City*, played poor Mary.)

Gossipy Sylvia Fowler (ROSALIND RUSSELL) shows off her "jungle red" nails to dear friend Mary Haines (NORMA SHEARER), though her true shade is green.

MGM, 1939

The Diana of the Hunt of the group, Joan Crawford, found a role that fit her like Spandex on Siegfried and Roy: that of the gold-digging, social-climbing shop girl, Crystal Allen. She is the wanton woman who snags Stephen from Mary, though not forever. When her newfound friends, who were Mary's old ones, finally grow envious of Crystal—for having found a stud of a boyfriend on the side—they turn on her.

"There's a name for you ladies," Crystal tells the women, after she's been clawed to pieces by them, "but it isn't used in high society—outside of a kennel."

Naturally, this is a total fantasy. Women aren't like that at all. That's why Bette Midler has said, "The worst part of success is to try finding someone who is happy for you."

Jealousy Cordial

Known as a Grasshopper before enraged Vegans complained.

1 ounce green crème de menthe
1 ounce white crème de cocoa or 1 oz. cream

Shake with ice and strain. Serve up in a champagne flute or goblet.
Ice cream may be substituted for the cream for a frozen variation.

This libation is particularly recommended for the jilted, as it magnifies the deficiencies you feel. In addition to which, when drunk in sufficient quantity, it will turn you so green and woozy that no one will need to ask how you feel.

Envy By the Book

If you are the lovers Anna Karenina and Count Vronsky, a jealous society will crush you even though it is inferior to you.

Tolstoy is bigger in Hollywood than one might think, even bigger than Deepak Chopra. Anna's sad tale has so far been told at least three times, first in a silent 1928 version called *Love* and starring the real-life off-screen lovers Greta Garbo and John Gilbert. David O. Selznick produced the 1935 remake, which used the novel's original name; Garbo again played Anna but this time Vronsky was Frederic March. Alexander Korda

GARBO was allowed to talk in her second *Anna Karenina*. "I'm so happy," Anna told her lover Vronksy (FREDRIC MARCH) in this scene. What a line! Say, doesn't she have a train to meet?

Her voice trembled in an ecstacy of happiness and love. "I'm so happy," she murmured.

A Metro-Goldwyn-Mayer PICTURE

Garbo · FREDRIC MARCH
ANNA KARENINA

PARAMOUNT, 1935

gave the story another go in 1948, with Vivien Leigh and Kieron Moore. Perhaps it is time to unite the tragic lovers once more. Angelina Jolie and Billy Bob Thornton, are you listening?

If you are Emma Bovary, a smug, provincial society will envy your romantic nature and adulterous adventures. But they won't forgive you even after you poison yourself.

No fewer than ten adaptations of Gustave Flaubert's *Madame Bovary* have made it to the screen—eleven, if one counts David Lean's transference of the tale to Ireland, which he called *Ryan's Daughter*. While no means perfect, Vincente Minnelli's 1949 MGM *Madame Bovary*, starring Jennifer Jones as the ill-fated Emma, is the most satisfying version, certainly more so than the excruciatingly dull Claude Chabrol 1991 take on the tale with Isabelle Huppert. Where's the MTV adaptation?

ENVY IN BLOOM

In Mel Brooks' *The Producers*, first in the 1968 movie version and then in the 2001 Broadway musical, it is envy that spurs timorous accountant Leo Bloom to follow the rhinoceros-like Max Bialystock into a scheme whereby they defraud investors while they attempt to mount the worst play ever seen on the Great White Way.

In the film (with the dialogue altered only slightly on stage), Max seduces Leo by pointing out the miserable existence that the numbers man leads, especially compared to the style in which other people live—including those whose money Leo counts. With the words, "There it

PLAYBILL®

ST. JAMES THEATRE

716

THE PRODUCERS
the new MEL BROOKS musical

WWW.PLAYBILL.COM

is, Bloom," Max tells Leo from the top of the Empire State Building (on stage, the exchange takes place in Max's office), "the most exciting city in the world. Thrills. Adventure. Romance. Everything you ever dreamed of is down there. Big black limousines. Gold cigarette cases. Elegant ladies with long legs."

Will Leo ultimately succumb to Max's scheme? After much searching of his conscience, he will. Leo screeches, "I want everything I've ever seen in the movies!"

The bicoastal and renewed success of Mel Brooks is so sensational and so deserved that it's (almost) impossible to be jealous of him.

Envy: A Who's Who

Diane Sawyer and Barbara Walters are friends.

Liz Smith and Cindy Adams are colleagues.

Montreal and Toronto are cities in Canada.

Looking Out For the Other Guy

"No story ever looks as bad as the story you've just bought; no story ever looks as good as the story that the other fellow just bought."
—FABLED MGM PRODUCTION CHIEF IRVING G. THALBERG (1899-1936)

"When I was a kid, we had *The Dirty Dozen* and *The Great Escape*. What do they have now? Fifty bad ones for every good one."
—MIRAMAX HONCHO HARVEY WEINSTEIN

Find the Envy Here

Madonna's British accent

"**F**ormer Warners potentate . . . Terry Semel last week took the helm of Yahoo, which is sort of like the ruler of an Arab emirate assuming leadership of a kibbutz. Yahoo is a sleeves-up, sandwiches-at-the-desk sort of company where executives take the red-eye to avoid paying hotel bills. In his former life, Semel wouldn't go from Burbank to Malibu without summoning the Warner's jet." —Peter Bart, *Variety*

Frank Sinatra, Jr.

Why the Carnation Was Green

"**I**t's not enough that I succeed. All my friends must also fail." —Oscar Wilde

Oh, What the Hell?

If you are Warren Beatty, you are used to the envy.

An Expanding Envy

"Penis Envy n. (ca. 1924): the supposed coveting of the penis by a young human female which is held in psychoanalytic theory to lead to feelings of inferiority or compensatory behavior." —*Webster's Ninth New Collegiate Dictionary*.

There is a school of thought that says it is penis envy, and not Hummers, that drives Hollywood. Why else is there competition every Monday morning to advertise the biggest gross of the weekend? The message: Mine is bigger than yours.

In the Golden Days of Hollywood, such blatant exhibitionism wasn't necessarily the case. Not that the moguls of yore were more gentlemanly than the producers of today. It's just that the weekly box office wasn't displayed as such a *shtupping* contest. The Goldwyns, the Mayers, the Warners, et. al, for all their faults, at least loved the movies. (By the 1970s, Joseph L. Mankiewicz was already saying that, compared to the Hollywood executive of the day, the men he worked for in the '40s and '50s were the Medicis.) To a Zanuck and a Harry Cohn, the audience was also a consideration. Today, it's not what the audience wants. It's not even (thank you, Sigmund) what women want. To the movie producer who is a member of a nearly exclusive male coterie, it's all about what I want.

Hollywood's Most-Wanted List

FOR THE PRODUCER: The bigger Bentley
FOR THE DIRECTOR: The bigger bungalow
FOR THE STAR: The bigger billing

Tennis Envy, Anyone?

In 1989, the Federal Communications Commission fined a Miami radio station for playing a song by a Seattle music group that called itself Uncle Bonsai. The song in question: "Penis Envy," a satire of macho attitudes on sitting in, stroking, straddling and stick-shifting sports cars. In retrospect the song's chief offense was that it was puerile, but it did prove that penis envy had entered the mainstream.

Radio schlock jock Howard Stern pushed the envelope on penis envy further when he openly admitted, first in his published memoir and then in its screen adaptation, *Private Parts*, that as an adolescent in his school locker room he went slack-jawed in envy of the equipment of his African-American classmates.

But leave it to comedian Tom Green to take penis envy to its unnatural conclusion. In his auteurist exercise, *Freddy Got Fingered*, Green was not content merely to play with himself. He masturbated an elephant.

Trans-Atlantic Envy

"Young man, there is America—which at this day serves for little more than to amuse you with stories of savage men and uncouth manners; yet shall, before you taste death, show itself equal to the whole of that commerce which now attracts the envy of the world." —EDMUND BURKE, 1775

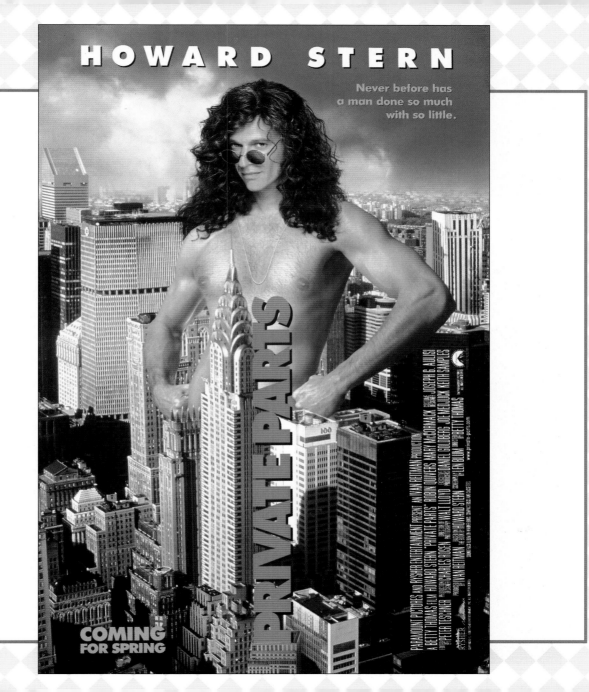

GENTLEMEN DON'T PREFER GREEN-EYED BLONDES

More than fifty years after her star rose, and nearly forty years after her death, Hollywood's greatest star is still Marilyn Monroe. Lives there a screen personality today who doesn't crave, if nothing else, Marilyn's long-lived legend?

In Marilyn's own time no rival better embodied this career jealousy than the buxom Jayne Mansfield, who was kept in the shadows by Marilyn's studio, Twentieth Century Fox, as insurance to keep Monroe in check. (Lauren Bacall was similarly threatened, it was said, by the lesser, though always available, Liszabeth Scott). After Marilyn died (at age thirty-six) in 1962,

Pretender Jayne Mansfield was never a match for Marilyn.

Mansfield allegedly told friends that it was a great career break for her.

Only it wasn't. The public mourned Marilyn, and Mansfield, who lacked Marilyn's charisma to begin with, was relegated to cheapie flicks produced in Europe—that is, until her own untimely death (at the age of thirty-four) in 1967.

What's Playing Out There?

Why the English Envy Americans:

1. Flouride
2. Showers
3. Central heating
4. Ice
5. Sunshine

Why Washingtonians Envy New Yorkers:

1. The Hamptons (Ever been to Rehoboth?)
2. *Their* mayors don't get thrown in jail.
3. *The New York Times*
4. Their proximity to Wall Street money
5. Home of *George* magazine . . . Oops!

Why New Yorkers Envy Angelenos:

1. They wear less clothing.
2. Big houses
3. Swimming pools 'n' movie stars
4. Cars (and places to park them)
5. The Sheen Boys

Why Angelenos envy Hawaiians:

1. They wear even less clothing.
2. Scenery
3. The air
4. Jack Nicholson is 3,000 miles away.
5. Macademia nuts/Don Ho (a tie)

Naked Envy: *A Man of the Sandwich Islands Dancing* by R.C. Barnfield, circa 1886, from a John Webber engraving

Self-Winding Jealousy

Judith Lieber evening bag, move over. The status accessory that guarantees envy in the movie enclave of Malibu goes tick, tick, tick—and it's not an interview on *60 Minutes*.

"We often desire goods not for the substantive benefits they confer but only for purposes of display and assertions of status—for what Veblen termed 'conspicuous consumption.' You can buy a serviceable wristwatch for $20, an excellent one for $200. But if you want to impress your friends, there's a Patek Philippe for $17,500. That is, if you're willing to settle for a regular production-run model. Should you really care to make a statement, a Patek Philippe Calibre '89, of which only four were manufactured, might dent your wallet for over $3 million."
—JACK HIRSHLEIFER, "Purchase Disorder," *Reason* magazine.

Jealousy, 1890, by Edvard Munch

Mine is Bigger Than Yours At Sea

Greek shipping magnates Stavros Niarchos (1908-1996) and Aristotle Onassis (1907-1975) carried on one of the more notorious rivalries of the twentieth century, and no possession better symbolized their competitive natures than their yachts. Whereas Onassis's Christina, named for his only daughter, was surpassed in length (by some fifty feet) by Niarchos's Atlantis, the Atlantis took a distinct backseat in the barstool department. On Ari's yacht the barstools were pure Studio City chic—covered with the buttery soft and incredibly expensive foreskin of the sperm-whale penis.

And you thought only Elvis had taste.

The Art

# of Making
Scenes

Blood is thicker than water—which makes it harder to clean up. Think of this the next time it crosses your mind to murder a relative. But why narrow your homicidal tendencies to members of your immediate family? The entertainment industry offers so many role models happy to show you how to make a scene anywhere you go.

After all, there's a great big wonderful world out there.

Stage Rage Returns

Rent is an angry musical. It is not *My Fair Lady*. The plays of Sam Shepard are angry. They are not *Private Lives*. The seminal force behind all this rage on stage in the second half of the 20th century was British playwright, screenwriter and memoirist John Osborne (1929-1994).

What made him so angry?

Osborne's father, an advertising copywriter in London, died before the boy's very eyes when John was only twelve. Insurance policy proceeds saw the melancholy John through Belmont College in Devon. Osborne, however, was no scholar. In fact, he left school after he had struck the headmaster.

Returning to London, Osborne lived briefly with his mother, a barmaid named Nellie Beatrice. His interest in theater was sparked when he took a job tutoring young performers on tour, and he graduated to become actor-manager for a string of repertory companies before deciding to try his hand at playwriting. In 1956, at the age of twenty-six, he presented his first

Alison (MARY URE) gets an earful of venom from Jimmy (RICHARD BURTON) in *Look Back in Anger*.

work, the acid-toned kitchen-sink drama *Look Back in Anger*.

Like many a freshman effort, it is a memory play, filled with self-referential scenes. Its most gut-wrenching speech concerns witnessing a loved one die. When it comes to family, the play's references are curdling—Osborne's way of getting back at his mother for being socially unacceptable.

After Osborne's death (of complications from diabetes), critic Richard Corliss wrote of the playwright's work, "This was drama as rant, an explosion of bad manners, a declaration of war against an empire in twilight."

And influential as all hell. Drama's new thrust—raw and real—sent Noel Coward into a genuine depression. He was not alone. "When I saw *Look Back in Anger*," said the genteel John Gielgud, also of the old school, "I thought my number was up."

The Brits made a movie of *Look Back in Anger* in 1958, but Hollywood didn't manage to catch up to Osborne's sense of realism for decades. Then it refused to release anger from its grip. By the 'eighties, a raw, ragged sensibility really took over popular American culture. Some blame *Raging Bull* (1980) for the bleak-out.

Fluff nearly has been banished entirely—

ANGER AND THE KING

If you are the King of Siam (YUL BRYNNER) and one of your slaves (RITA MORENO) has run off with her lover, repressing your rage will appease your children's governess (DEBORAH KERR) but will break your own spirit, sending you to an early death while an off-screen chorus sings "Song of the King."

replaced by gross-out teen flicks, either of the slasher or of the scatological humor variety—and politeness and good manners on screen are . . . gone with the wind.

This pisses off a good many people.

The King (YUL BRYNNER) hopes to take it—his anger—with him. Anna (DEBORAH KERR) hopes to argue him out of this, too.

The King and I, Twentieth Century Fox, 1956

SPILLOVER ANGER

"Brutal underground 'fight clubs'; similar to the one featured in the film starring Brad Pitt are being set up across the UK, according to an investigation.

"Extreme no-rules fighting contests at warehouses, behind pubs, on gypsy camps and at a clearing in Epping Forest, Essex, have been discovered.

"Contenders earn around £100 a fight, and can use disciplines including kung-fu, karate, wrestling and kick boxing.

"A report today looks at the proliferation of such clubs in the U.K. and the influence of the film, *Fight Club*, which was a massive box-office success.

"It also cites a case in the Ukraine where a 'fight club' member was killed in the ring after having his head smashed onto the canvas fourteen times.

"In the movie, Pitt plays a character who sets up an underground club where disillusioned Americans can come and vent their frustrations by fighting each other in bouts without rules.

"The real fight clubs are increasingly being advertised on the Internet."
—BRITISH PRESS ASSOCIATION

Film Review

James Cameron-Wilson

" How much can you really know about yourself
if you've never been in a fight?"
-Tyler Durden

FIGHT CLUB

One Angry Actor (Off Screen)

The New York Post and Alec Baldwin despise one another. The actor sees red over the tabloid's right-wing politics and its repeated reference to how "bloated" Baldwin looks; the *Post* sees purple over being criticized by Baldwin on the *Late Show with David Letterman*.

But the temper on Alec goes beyond politics, according to news reports. Street-side witnesses told the *Post* that they saw the actor go ballistic in Manhattan and toss his cell phone against a wall. Then, hurling expletives, Alec supposedly stomped the device to smithereens.

Yet say what you want about Baldwin, a litterbug he's not. Witnesses said that the actor picked up the pieces of his phone and stuffed them in his pocket, before walking away.

Why Johnny Fumes

America is just too angry for Johnny Depp. That's why, he has said, that he and his girlfriend, actress Vanessa Paradis, live in France.

This seems a bit of a stretch for the Kentucky-born leading man, who is no stranger to playing tough guys (in *Donnie Brasco* and *Blow*). He also has had real-life angry blowups. In 1989, police in Vancouver, B.C., charged him with assault in connection with a fight with a hotel security guard. A decade later, Depp was arrested in London for fighting with paparazzi outside a restaurant.

Still, Depp told the Associated Press that he is *shocked* by what he sees when he returns to the United States, now that he and Paradis have a daughter, Lily-Rose Melody. "I mean," Depp said, "little kids going into school and shooting up their pals and killing people. I have a little girl . . . I don't want her to grow up with that kind of thing in her brain."

Now, that's a responsible parent.

"Never wrestle with a pig. You just get dirty, and the pig enjoys it."
—George Bernard Shaw

The Night He Didn't Love Lucy

If you are Ricky Ricardo and your wife, Lucy, has severed your contract with MGM by pretending to be your agent and antagonizing studio chief Dore Schary, thus making you the most angry you have ever been at her, you smash an ashtray, utter a long rant in Spanish, then disappear for the night.

But the Crock Pot Was There

Bad-boy rocker Tommy Lee insists that his bust-up with beach bunny Pamela Anderson started over a misplaced frying pan. The former Motley Crue drummer confessed to *Rolling Stone* that he had attacked his wife because he couldn't find his favorite cooking utensil.

"Pamela came over, saw that I was in one of those moods, and just threw up her hands and said, ''Calm down, it's just a pan.'"

Lee's rare burst of introspection came after cooling out four months in a Malibu jail. "I should have walked outside and just vented at the stars or gone for a jog or taken a cold shower," he said, "but I didn't."

Hip-Hopping Mad — Part One

Hip-hop artist Eminem, whose real name is Marshall Bruce Mathers III, pleaded guilty to misdemeanors, in February 2001, after prosecutors agreed to drop the felony assault charge filed after he allegedly pistol-whipped a man he saw kissing his wife, Kimberly Mathers. Eminem's reputed pique of jealousy had raged in the parking lot of a suburban Detroit music club in the late hours of night.

The Grammy-winning musician, who routinely poses for press photographers while flipping the bird, is known for lyrics so misogynist that even his mother and wife are outraged—both have sued him over what he has said about them in albums. (Mom, in fact, asked for $11 million in her legal action against her son. She settled for $25,000.)

In April 2001, Macomb County (Mich.) Judge Antonio Viviano sentenced Eminem to two years' probation, warning him that he could face up to five years in prison for any violation of the terms of the sentence. "I consider probation to be punishment. I don't think it's a lark, and I don't think it's a slap on the wrist," the judge said.

Two months later, another jurist slapped another year's probation on the musician, this time in connection with his "no contest" plea after being charged with brandishing a 9mm semiautomatic gun during an alleged dispute with Douglas Dail, a member of the rival Detroit rap group Insane Clown Posse. "The activity you engaged in will not be tolerated in a civilized society," Circuit Judge Denise Langford Morris told the celebrated alleged gunslinger at the time of his sentencing.

In both cases, Eminem, on the advice of his attorneys, kept his mouth shut and his finger to himself.

Annals of Travel— Road Rage

Driver Andrew Burnett allegedly reacted to a Northern California fender bender by grabbing a small dog from the offending car, and throwing the pet into ongoing traffic, where it was killed. "It was like lightning," said Sara McBurnett, the dog's owner.

Hip-Hopping Mad – Part Two

Dramatis Personae: Rap music mogul (Bad Boy Records) Sean "Puff Daddy" Combs, his girlfriend Jennifer Lopez ("J Lo"), Combs's protégé Jamal Shyne Barrow, Combs's bodyguard Anthony "Wolf" Jones and club-goer, Matthew "Scar" Allen.

Act I

Setting: INTERIOR Club New York, Manhattan

Large detail from Atlas Puncture Proof, 911

Time: December 27, 1999
A dispute between Puffy and Scars leads to an exchange of angry words, some having to do with mothers and reproductive functions. A person or persons fire(s) shots into the air. Bullet fragments wound three people.

EXTERIOR Club New York
Same night
Shyne is arrested with a firearm in his waistband.

EXT. City Streets
Minutes Later
Police pursue Lincoln Navigator containing Combs, J Lo, Wolf and a driver. Navigator stops. Police retrieve one gun from the car and find another outside the

Fights to please fans used to have referees: *Stag at Sharkey's*, 1909, by George Bellows

Annals of Travel — Air Rage

In March of 2001, a New Jersey jury decided that passenger John Davis Jr. had not behaved criminally in a 1999 assault that broke the neck of a Continental Airlines airport-gate agent.

Davis apparently convinced jurors that he was acting in self-defense. The agent, Angelo Scottile (some 20 years older than Davis) had run out of boarding passes, so Davis's wife and young daughter rushed to the plane without them—so eager were they to fly to Orlando to visit Disney World. Davis, angered by Scottile's attempt to stop his family, reportedly picked up the agent and slammed him to the ground.

As it turned out, the Davis family did not fly to Disney World that day. But they drove there in 2000. No word on what was their favorite ride.

club. (One witness will later testify that this gun was thrown from the Lincoln. Trash talk will also surface, accusing Puffy of trying to bribe the driver into saying gun was his.)

INT. Police Station
Puffy is booked for unauthorized gun possession and attempted bribery of a witness. Wolf is booked on the same charges.

Shyne is charged with first degree assault and depraved indifference to human life, as well as criminal possession of a gun.

Intermission

Puffy prepares for trial by launching a clothing line, Sean Jean.

Shyne and Wolf lie low.

Scar disappears under a cloud of suspicion that is never explained.

J Lo appears nearly naked at the Grammys before going to Australia on a concert tour, saying that she will willingly appear in court to defend Combs's innocence. And, not to be outdone in the thread game, she launches her own clothing line, Sweetheart Fashion. On Valentine's Day, 2000, representatives for the couple say that Puffy and J Lo have broken up.

The press wonders if there will be an audience for Act II.

Act II:

INT. Courtroom, New York State Superior Court
January-March 2001
At the trial, Puffy's wardrobe commands more attention than

Masking anger is a lost art: *Les Fetiches*, 1905, by Lõis Mailou Jones

the prosecution witnesses (whose outfits clash). On account of his good taste (some say), Puffy is acquitted. So is Wolf, though no one remarks on his wardrobe.

Shyne is found depraved and guilty. (Attorney Johnnie Cochran—whose fashion taste is faultless—goes on the *Today* show and says the verdict is a crime because Shyne's music career was just taking off.)

EXT. Courthouse
Puffy gives interviews to *Time*, *The New York Times* and *Newsday* (for the suburban audience), declaring that he thanks God and is changing his name to "P. Diddy."

Epilogue
Own your own record empire before losing your temper.

Hip-Hopping Mad— Part Three

NYPD officers blamed bad blood between hardcore hip-hopsters Lil' Kim (oh, she also of so lil' clothing at the Grammys) and Capone-N-Noreaga for a February 2001 shootout outside a Greenwich Village radio station, Hot 97, in which pals of both "entertainers" had appeared.

Police said some 22 rounds of ammunitions were fired, and one man (said to be with the Capone contingent) went down on the sidewalk before the shooters fled.

To be frank about this, the whole saga is both confusing and tiresome.

For the record, managers for both Capone-N-Noreaga and Lil' Kim said their clients were not at the crime scene.

What Was Playing in Columbine

The videogame, "Doom," was a particular favorite of one Colorado high school student, who reprogrammed its locale to look like his own neighborhood—Columbine—before he and a friend translated their killing fantasies to live action at their school.

U.S. Attorney General John Ashcroft has also cited another game, "Dope Wars," as contributing to what he describes as "the culture of violence" influencing angry teens. Although the "Dope Wars" website is supposedly closed to minors, the down-loadable game is described as "low-tech but high fun." Players become debt-ridden drug dealers who try to find profit while dodging the police and muggers.

Ashcroft would like parents to monitor their offspring's entertainment.

And then what? Switch them to *Oz*.

Anger on the Rocks

Also known as *El Toro Sangriento*—translation: Bloody Bull—a far more fiery concoction than an ordinary vodka Bloody Bull.

1 jigger (ounce) tequila gold
3 ounces tomato juice
3 ounces beef consommé
Several dashes Worcestershire sauce
Pinch of celery salt (optional)
Pinch of white pepper

Irately mix all the ingredients with cracked ice, and serve in a double old-fashioned glass. Garnish rim with a slice of lemon or lime.

    Should the alcoholic content of the above not do the trick, this drink contains enough sodium to boost *anyone's* blood pressure and allow the fuse to blow, as it were.

Night Town by William Mulhall

What's Playing in Wilmington?

"One's too many, and a hundred's not enough."
—bartender in *The Lost Weekend*

Pan to Spring, 2001, in scenic Wilmington, N. C., where production is taking place on the movie, *Domestic Disturbance*. But offstage, a real drama is brewing. Two-shot of screenwriter Scott Rosenberg and actor Vince Vaughn having a drink at the scruffy Firebelly Lounge. Another cast member, Steve Buscemi (*Fargo*), is b.g.

Wide shots. A strange woman allegedly walks up to Vaughn. She may have seen him before—he played Norman Bates in the *Psycho* remake. A melee breaks lose. Exactly what happened isn't clear. But Buscemi, is left with stab wounds to the throat and head.

According to the *Wilmington Morning Star*, one Timothy William Fogerty, of Wilmington, was charged with assault with a deadly weapon with intent to kill for allegedly stabbing Buscemi.

As Fogerty is being led away in handcuffs, Vaughn, Rosenberg and a Wilmington local resume the argument, and the police haul them away, too.

It's enough to make one yearn for the relative calm of Fargo, N.D.

ANGER: A WHO'S WHO

Contrary to popular belief:

Laurel and Hardy did not hate each other.
Abbott and Costello did not hate each other.
However, Curly had issues with Moe.

TWO INNOCENT
SAILORS ON A
HOLIDAY.... BUT
THEY ENDED UP
ALL AT SEA.....

Stan
LAUREL
Oliver
HARDY
in
'OUR
RELATIONS'

A Metro-
Goldwyn

Facing page: Real-life brothers CURLY and MOE HOWARD
(the two Stooges on the left) could have starred in *It's a
Mad, Mad, Mad, Mad World*.

ABBOTT and COSTELLO (above) and LAUREL and HARDY
(left) could not.

Casting Call for Ma Barker

The bride wore a bulletproof vest. So did the groom, the priest and the Terre Haute, Indiana, wedding planner.

Apparently, the prospective mother-in-law did not care for her son's intended, and had told him in no uncertain terms, "If you marry her, I'm going to come in and blow you all away."

No one had taken Mother seriously—until she showed up at a relative's funeral, where she slapped the corpse and slammed the lid of the casket. Then Mom kicked the funeral director and broke his leg in three places.

The day before her son's wedding, she called the rectory five times and threatened the clergyman with bodily harm.

The morning of the happy event itself, the nervous groom called home and ordered his mother to stay away. "She didn't show," wedding planner Teddy Lenderman later told *The New York Times*.

As for the bride and groom, shaken but not stirred, they made it safely to their honeymoon hideaway.

Why There Will Always Be An England

"To fight like two middle-class educated Englishmen would fight, which I've always maintained would be girly, cowardly—with squealing."
—HUGH GRANT on why he and Colin Firth duke it out like wimps in *Bridget Jones's Diary*

Why Goldie No Longer Sleeps with the Fishes

"A diner at a curry house reached into one of the restaurant's fish tanks and hurled a goldfish across the room, killing it instantly, because, he said, it had been bullying the other occupants of the tank.

"Anwar Ali, 27, a waiter at the Royal Curry Tandoori restaurant in Gloucester, saw the goldfish bounce off a table leg on the other side of the restaurant. 'We were very upset because we liked that fish. We had it for more than a year,' he said."
—BRITISH PRESS ASSOCIATION

The Anger Catalog

If you are a Montague, then you hate the Capulets.
If you are a Capulet, then you hate the Montagues.
If you are a Shark, then you hate the Jets.
If you are a Jet, then you hate the Sharks.
If you are a Buddhist, you love all of the above.

CHAPTER FOUR

Lines Etched

In Acid

One picture is worth a thousand words—which means these insults from three-quarters of a century worth of motion pictures speak volumes. And speaking of volume, while repeating any of the following, please belt it out like Ethel Merman. Remember her? Thought not. Dummy.

CHARM

"Awwwwwwwwwwww."
—Tom Powers (JAMES CAGNEY) in the face of Kitty (MAE CLARK) in *The Public Enemy*

WARNER BROS., 1931

PARAMOUNT, 1933

UNIVERSAL, 1940

ELOQUENCE

"I'm a man of one word: Scram!"—Rufus T. Firefly (GROUCHO MARX) in *Duck Soup*

REASON

"Well, she's not going to tell me I don't love her." —Edgar Souse (W.C. FIELDS) after his mother-in-law, Myrtle (UNA MERKEL), tells him not to strike his daughter in *The Bank Dick*

TRUTH

"You're a descendant of generations of inbred, incestuous mental defectives. How dare you call anyone barbarian!"—Julius Caesar (REX HARRISON) to the Queen of the Nile (ELIZABETH TAYLOR) in *Cleopatra*

"Stronger than all my afterthoughts is my fury." —*Hippolytus* by EURIPIDES

TWENTIETH CENTURY FOX, 1963

JUSTICE

"I'll get you, my pretty, and your little dog, too!" The Wicked Witch of the West (MARGARET HAMILTON) to Dorothy (JUDY GARLAND) in *The Wizard of Oz*.

MGM, 1939

THE AMERICAN WAY

"Get out, Veda. Get your things out of this house right now before I throw them into the street and you with them. Get out before I kill you." —Mother (JOAN CRAWFORD) to her daughter (ANN BLYTH) in *Mildred Pierce*

WARNER BROTHERS, 1945

CLARIFICATION

"I don't bray!" —Martha (ELIZABETH TAYLOR) to George (RICHARD BURTON) in *Who's Afraid of Virginia Woolf?*

SELZNICK INTERNATIONAL, 1937

SKILL

" I'm sitting here, Mr. Cook, toying with the idea of removing your heart—and stuffing it like an olive." —Newspaper editor Oliver Stone (WILLIAM CONNOLLY) raging at a reporter, Wally Cook (FREDRIC MARCH), as Hazel Flagg (CAROLE LOMBARD) comes between them in *Nothing Sacred*

COURTESY

" Would you do me a favor, Harry? . . . Drop dead!" —Billie Dawn (JUDY HOLLIDAY) to Harry Brock (BRODERICK CRAWFORD) in *Born Yesterday*

COLUMBIA, 1953

Laugh and the Mob Laughs, Too

Henry Hill (Ray Liotta): "You're really funny, you're . . ."

Tommy DeVito (Joe Pesci): "What do you mean, 'Really funny?'"

Hill: "You know, you're a funny guy."

DeVito: "You mean, the way I talk?"

Hill: "Just . . . just, you . . . the way you tell a story and everything."

DeVito: "'Funny,' how? I mean, what's funny about me?"

Hill (really on the spot): "Just . . ."

DeVito: "What?"

Hill: Just . . . you know, you're just funny."

DeVito: "Let me understand you. Maybe it's me . . . but funny how? I mean, I'm funny, what? I'm like a clown? I make you laugh? I amuse you? . . . How do I amuse you? You mean . . ."

Hill: "Just . . . you know."

DeVito: "No, I don't. Tell me what's funny . . ."

[dead silence]

Hill: "Get the f— outta here, Tommy."

DeVito (laughing): "I almost had him going."

—*GoodFellas* by Nicholas Pileggi

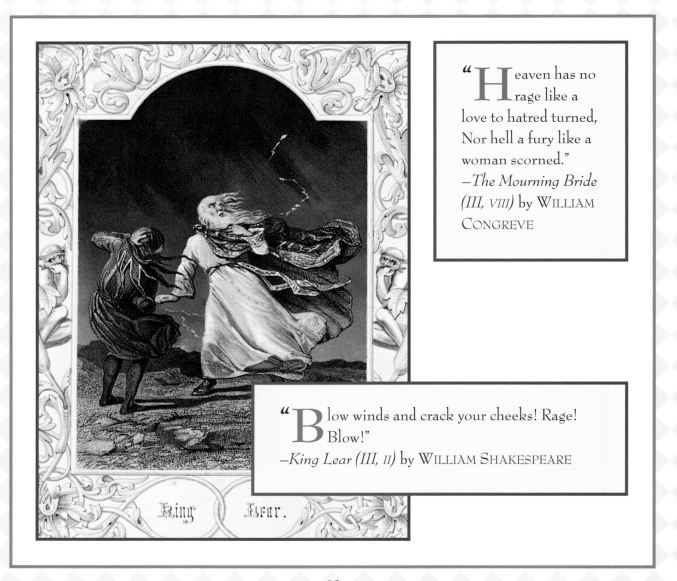

King Lear.

"Heaven has no rage like a love to hatred turned, Nor hell a fury like a woman scorned."
—*The Mourning Bride (III, VIII)* by WILLIAM CONGREVE

"Blow winds and crack your cheeks! Rage! Blow!"
—*King Lear (III, II)* by WILLIAM SHAKESPEARE

CHAPTER FIVE

How Sweet

It Is

"Don't get mad," Ivana Trump advises the characters played by BETTE MIDDLER, DIANE KEATON and GOLDIE HAWN in *The First Wives Club*. "Get everything."

The famous New Yorker (who is famous for being famous and for having been married and divorced from the famous Donald Trump) knew what she was talking about.

Ah, if only Calpurnia (aka Mrs. Ceasar) hadn't been above reproach. Had she hired a good divorce lawyer after her husband's very public dalliance with Cleopatra, all of ancient Rome could have been hers. Or, if she'd lived in California, at least fifty per cent.

Revenge in Ancient Troy

Sounds like the opening of a Julia Roberts movie: Eris (the goddess of Discord) is so upset at not having been invited to a chum's wedding, she decides to come anyway, bearing an apple, inscribed "For the Fairest."

Three wedding guests—Aphrodite, Athena and Hera (goddesses, all)—leap at the fruit, each confident that its message is intended for her. The great studio mogul, Zeus, knows better than to get his hands dirty with *this* one—these three beauties are his relatives! He delegates the choice to the Trojan prince, Paris, whose mortal life isn't worth much, anyhow.

Aphrodite gets to Paris, promising him that if she is chosen, she will reward him with the most beautiful mortal on earth—Helen.

Paris grabs the deal, and that is how the babe becomes known as Helen of Troy and goes on to launch a thousand ships. In NC-17 rated versions, Paris rapes and abducts her.

Bette **MIDLER** Goldie **HAWN** Diane **KEATON**

The
FIRST WIVES
Club

Don't get mad. Get everything.

But it's true love, nonetheless: Paris clearly awakens something in Helen that slept through her marriage to the Greek King Menelaus. This is all the more reason for jealous Menelaus to rouse the Greeks to a ten-year war on Troy, during which, incidentally, Achilles gets his (in the heel).

Victory finally finds the Greeks, through the special effect of a huge, wooden horse filled with soldiers. By this time, the Trojans are so worn out that they accept the object as a peace offering. (Beware of worn Trojans.)

In the end, Helen, looking ravishing for her age, returns to her lawful mate—which also sounds like the end of a Julia Roberts movie.

WARNER BROS.

THE FACE THAT LAUNCHED A THOUSAND SHIPS!

"Helen of Troy"

The tumultuous events that brought the Age of Titans to its raging climax! The spectacular Spartan siege set off by Helen and Paris, history's most famous runaway lovers!

In CINEMASCOPE AND WARNERCOLOR

3 years in the making at a cost of $6,000,000!

PERIOD REVENGE

Sweet is revenge, especially to women.
—*Don Juan* by LORD BYRON.

A scorned Newport Beach, Ca., woman of the '70s, sneaked into her ex-boyfriend's apartment, left water rings on his wooden speakers and switched the dust jackets on all 1,728 of his record albums.

Technical Note: This can work with DVDS, CDS or the complete works of John Grisham.

Revenge in Ancient Rome

Revenge can even foment rebellion. Consider the Rape of Lucretia (509 B.C.). The incident, which inspired an opera by Benjamin Britten, (Lucretia is an alto), revolves around a bet made by three Roman officers—Collatinus, Junius and Prince Tarquinius—as to which of their wives would remain faithful while they were away at war.

Only Lucretia, wife of Collatinus, remains true to her man. Prince Tarquinius, one sore loser, gallops back to Rome and rapes Lucretia. Overcome by shame, Lucretia commits suicide.

But to some observers, Cicero among them, this was not necessarily a bad thing, since in this case jealousy and revenge led to the replacement of capricious kings by capricious consuls. Cicero commented, "Lucretia, having been ravished by force by the king's son, and having invoked the citizens to avenge her, slew herself. And this indignation of hers was the cause of liberty to the state."

Revenge in Olde England

If you are Mordred, the bastard son of King Arthur (who is otherwise childless), and the cuckolded king refuses to recognize you as his heir, you begin a whispering campaign about Queen Guinevere's dalliance with Sir Lancelot, forcing Lancelot's Round Table cronies to take one of two dangerous positions: speak up or remain silent. The only glitch in your plan is that should the knights divide into factions and brandish their swords o'er the land, there won't be much left of a kingdom for you to rule. Besides, Arthur will go down in legend as a shining hero, while you will be known as the destroyer of Camelot.

Revenge in Olde Denmark

Hamlet seeks revenge on his stepfather, Claudius, for having married Hamlet's mother so soon after the death of Hamlet's father, but, as with so many issues in his life, Hamlet vacillates. Then again, he has ample cause—to vacillate, that is.

In the beginning, Hamlet has no evidence to suspect Claudius of treason; Claudius' worst sin may be bad timing. Hamlet is only convinced that his stepfather is a killer when a ghost comes along. Say, you'd hesitate, too. In some quarters, it's also whispered that Hamlet lost a lot of time because he had this thing for codpieces.

Even after it appears that no jury in Copenhagen would convict Hamlet, he waffles. An eye for an eye is not Hamlet's style. Furthermore, Hamlet is obliged by his personal demons to hesitate until the time is right to do away with Claudius. And even then, Hamlet senses that he has blown the entire operation. Hamlet is right. Hamlet is dead meat—literally.

Perhaps, Hamlet is not the best role model for revenge seekers. As Shakespearean heroes go, Othello was far more efficient—even if he failed to get the facts straight before he acted. Still, he did go on to be a Verdi opera.

Revenge in Olde Hollywood — Part I

Charles Lederer, who co-wrote *Kismet*, got ticked off when RKO studio boss Howard Hughes refused to give Lederer and his writing partner, Ben Hecht, a new screenwriting assignment unless they paid back a fee they'd received for a script that was never made.

Although most screenplay writers had to take that kind of treatment lying down, Lederer had a secret weapon: his sweet aunt, Marion Davies, who happened to be the lover of publisher William Randolph Hearst.

Davies wired Hughes: "Howard, is it true that you're going to give back to the American taxpayers all the money they paid you for that big flying boat that never flew? If so, it'll be a big story in all of W.R.'s papers."

Hughes got the hint. Lederer and Hecht got the job.

The Secret Weapon: MARION DAVIES

COSMOPOLITAN, 1936

99

REVENGE IN OLDE HOLLYWOOD — PART II

Another doublecross, another plot. This time Charles Lederer got mad at MGM producer Sam Zimbalist, but waited to hatch his little scheme until Zimbalist and his wife were away from their Bel Air home, skiing over Christmas.

Lederer then placed an ad in a Los Angeles paper: "Will Buy Used Xmas Trees After Xmas, Will Pay One to Ten Dollars Depending on Size, Leave on Lawn at [Zimbalist's address], Tagged with Your Name and Address to Which to Send the Money."
Many responded . . . then grew irate when Zimbalist didn't.

REVENGE IN OLDE HOLLYWOOD — PART III

Mia Farrow's father, John Farrow, was known as a mediocre movie director but a sensational womanizer. Not a nice one, mind you, he was a master of the love 'em and leave 'em school. And so many in old Hollywood took special relish in the story of one Farrow conquest, who got some of her own back. One day she caught up with the errant John at a red light. Catching his eye in his mirror, she gestured for him to follow her, which he did in hope of an impromptu lovemaking reprise.

At the lady's apartment, Farrow quickly undressed, but before pouncing on his hostess, he headed into the bathroom. She seized the moment to lock him inside, take his clothes, rip out the phone—and depart.

The Best Revenge Is Hamlet

Juvenile Court Judge Paul Perachi threw the play at a bunch of Pittsfield, Mass., teenagers who had occupied their idle hours with various pranks, including assault with a deadly weapon. Hizzoner ordered them to participate in a local production of *Hamlet* as part of their probation.

"What happens to these kids tomorrow—who knows?" the jurist later admitted to the Associated Press. But he maintained that his dramatic sentence gave the delinquents "the tools to communicate and hopefully make better decisions."

Nate, the fifteen-year-old who played the homicidal Claudius (on stage), had a confession of his own for the press: "I thought this was stupid at first, and I thought I would quit. But I'm proud of myself, I've never done anything all the way, through."

REVENGE IN OLDE HOLLYWOOD – FINALE ULTIMO

Joan Crawford and Bette Davis, both under contract to Warner Brothers, never liked each other. No love was gained when they made *What Ever Happened to Baby Jane?* in their early-twilight years.

Crawford was still a STAR but Bette Davis, who was always the better actress of the two, was nominated as Best Actress for her Betty Jane role. Crawford was nominated for nothing—but she nevertheless showed up on Oscar night at the Santa Monica Civic Auditorium, where she stood backstage, dispensing champagne from Pepsi-Cola coolers.

Best Actress was announced—and Anne Bancroft won the Oscar for her performance in *The Miracle Worker*.

But Bancroft couldn't accept the statuette, because she was in a play in New York. So that left Bette Davis to seethe as a spectator—while Joan Crawford came on stage to accept Bancroft's Oscar.

BETTE DAVIS won the battle of egos in *Whatever Happened to Baby Jane?* but lost the war on Oscar night.

REVENGE IN NEW HOLLYWOOD

Fatal Attraction is essentially an old-fashioned romance. After all, the villain does get punished at the end. That would be the Michael Douglas character, who is left with a wife who will never understand. Glenn Close also starred.

REVENGE IN THE TABLOIDS (EXPLAINED)

"Right after the divorce announcement, there's a story about Tom [Cruise] being broken hearted because Nicole [Kidman] left. The following week, there's Nicole's story on how she lost the baby and Tom doesn't care. They're going for sympathy, so the next time they're on a movie screen, you don't look at them and say, 'How can I believe him?'

"Remember, sixty percent of movie-ticket buyers are women, so a guy like Cruise doesn't want to turn off the woman in the Midwest who swoons when she sees him. It's all about bank-ability, acceptability and morality."
—DIVORCE ATTORNEY DOMINICK BARBARA

Revenge by the Book – Part I

If you are Catherine Earnshaw and you wish to teach a lesson to the roughhewn but romantic Heathcliffe, you marry your dandy neighbor, Edgar Linton.

If you are Heathcliffe and your beloved, tempestuous Cathy marries the foppish Edgar Linton, you marry his sister, Isabella Linton.

Literary Note: Nobody lives happily ever after.

Revenge by the Book – Part II

If you are Miss Havisham and have been jilted on your wedding day, you shall wreak your revenge on all members of the male sex by rearing your beautiful young ward, Estella, to treat all men both seductively and abominably. You will also never remove your wedding dress, though what harm that could possibly do to other people, save for the business of the local dry cleaner, is beyond comprehension.

Revenge by the Book — Part III

If you are Scarlett O'Hara and your beau, Ashley Wilkes, ups and marries his cousin, Melanie Hamilton, you marry Melanie's hapless brother, Charles. You then attach yourself to Melanie, solely for the purpose of breaking up her marriage.

Cinematic Note: Nobody lives happily ever after Scarlett's wedding, but the audience still has a long way to go. And, by the way, if you are the author Alice Randall and you wish to avenge the patronizing attitude of whites toward blacks in *Gone with the Wind*, you write *The Wind Done Gone*. And then, if you manage the Margaret Mitchell estate and you wish to get even with Randall, you go to court to try to stop *Done Gone* from getting published.

Finally, if you are Randall and you read the reveiws of *Done Gone*, well, frankly, my dear, you don't give a damn.

The *GWTW* revenge marriage everyone (including the bride) forgets: Scarlett (VIVIEN LEIGH) takes Charles (RAND BROOKS).

Revenge by the Book — Part IV

If you are Don Vito Corleone, and your godson, the popular singer Johnny Fontanne, wants a particular part in a serious war picture but is being thwarted in his casting quest by the studio's despotic owner, Jack Woltz, you dispatch your henchmen to find the prized thoroughbred horse belonging to the mogul and you . . . oh, just forget it. By now, that's *such* a cliché.

PARAMOUNT, 1972

This horse needed a godfather of his own.

EXTREME REVENGE

The verb "Bobbitt" entered the pop-culture lexicon in 1993 when John Wayne Bobbitt had unwilling benefit of this surgical procedure at the hands of his manicurist wife, Lorena. She resorted to this operation (presumably after practicing on hangnails), she said, in retaliation for her husband's abuse and infidelities. The instrument she used was the kitchen knife.

Bobbitt, who was able to have his organ surgically reattached, also retains, by dint of personal effort, his notoriety. Recently, he announced from his Las Vegas residence that he planned to file a court motion to retrieve the famous weapon—in hopes he might sell it on eBay. The red-handled twelve-inch knife reportedly has remained all these years in the custody of the Prince William County, Va., police.

REVENGE BY THE BOOK – PART V

If you are Christina Crawford and wish to get back at your mother, Joan (See "Revenge in Olde Hollywood, Finale Ultimo"), for cutting you out of her will, you write *Mommie Dearest*.

If you are Gary Crosby and wish to get back at your father, Bing, for roughing you up and calling you fat, you write *Going My Own Way*.

If you are Rock Brynner and wish to get back at your father, Yul, for being cold and detached, you write *Yul: The Man Who Would be King*.

If you are Maxine Marx and wish to get back at your father, Groucho, for being like Yul Brynner, you write *Growing Up with Groucho*.

If you are William Berle and wish to get back at your father, Milton, for being like Groucho, you write *My Father, Uncle Miltie*.

If you are B. D. Hyman and wish to get back at your mother, Bette Davis, for being not better in the motherhood department than Joan Crawford was, you write *My Mother's Keeper*.

If you are Lorna Luft and wish to get back at the world because your mother was Judy Garland and your half-sister is Liza Minnelli, you write *Me and My Shadows: A Family Memoir*, and then serve as executive producer when the book is turned into an ABC Movie of the Week.

After Christina Crawford got even with Joan Crawford in print and on screen, Mother's Day was never the same.

PARAMOUNT, 1983

Also Out of the Mouth of Babes

What does a Hollywood brat give his dad for Father's Day? A subpoena.

It worked for Macaulay Culkin, who obviously learned a thing or two while doing all those Home Alone movies. When he was seventeen, he got even with his father, Kit Culkin, who managed the young actor's career, by cutting him off. "He was a domineering man," the young actor later told interviewers. "Not so much physical, though, there was a bit of that. It was mental abuse."

The elder Culkin (who had been a relatively unsuccessful actor himself) kept his son's movie projects coming, even when Junior wanted a break. "I wanted a summer vacation for the first time in, you know, forever," Macaulay remembered. His dad nixed it.

After the young actor retrieved $17 million of his earnings, his wounded dad left the scene, which, incidentally included six other children.

Grammy-winning country singer Le Ann

ARTVILLE

Cat & Canary by Stephen F. Hayes

Rimes also went to court, at sour seventeen, with a brief against her manager/dad, Wilbur Rimes, alleging that he had misappropriated $7 million of her royalties.

When a Nashville judge, in 2001, rejected LeAnn's bid to end a recording contract her father had negotiated for her when she was twelve, the singer, by then eighteen, burst into tears and yelled at her father, "I hate you."

Speaking to reporters later, her father sighed, "She's acting like a spoiled brat."

Revenge Comedy

Cast: Big man Jackie Gleason (1916-1987) and Broadway impresario David Merrick (1911-2000).

Time: 1959.

Setting: The Great White Way, with "The Great One" (Gleason) starring in the musical *Take Me Along* for "The Abominable Showman" (Merrick).

When Gleason missed a performance, claiming a stomachache, Merrick told the press, "I sympathize with Jackie, because when he has a stomachache, it's like a giraffe having a sore throat."

Gleason's comeback: "Merrick," he told reporters, "really believes I had a stomachache, because he gives one to everyone near him."

Merrick: "My mother told me never to have anything to do with actors."

Gleason's curtain line: "He loves money so much that he ignored his mother's advice."

REVENGE ON HBO

If you are Mafia princess Janice Soprano, the sister of godfather Tony, and your late mother's caregiver refuses to turn over mom's collection of vintage original cast albums that she claims the old lady had left to her, you urgently explain to the employee that you wish to have the LPs returned *tutti pronti*.

You also tenderly underscore the emotional attachment you felt toward the matriarch and how those show albums represented her. And when the caregiver still refuses to comply with your wish, you wait until she is asleep—and then steal her prosthetic leg. (Proviso: Insure beforehand that the caregiver has no connections with the Russian Mob and therefore is capable of extracting her own sweet revenge.)

CLEAN REVENGE

If you are Barbra Streisand, and your co-star, Walter Matthau, has told you, "I have more talent in my smallest fart than you have in your entire body," you hand him a bar of soap to wash out his mouth.

MESSY REVENGE

One of the more polite vengeful acts pulled by the usually volatile Frank Sinatra was perpetrated on insult-comic Don Rickles. Ol' Blue Eyes was not pleased by the Rickles' nightclub quip, "Hey Frank, why don't you make yourself at home—beat up somebody."

Sinatra let that ride. But he was further displeased by a later Rickles' crack about Frank's needing to give his kids work, specifically Rickles' line about daughter Nancy Sinatra's singing talents.

Sinatra did not break any of Rickles' bones, however.

Instead, the Chairman of the Board had his entire entourage fill all the front seats at a Rickles' performance. Then, came a signal from the man himself, and everybody let fly at Rickles' face a cream pie.

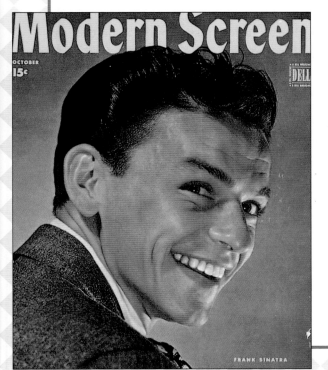

MONEY IS THE BEST REVENGE

If you are David Letterman, and NBC does not hand over the reins of the *Tonight* show to you, you jump ship to CBS for $24 million a year.

Killer Chocolate Milk

If you're a Baby Boomer, this playground parody of a popular commercial jingle for a chocolate-like syrup may trigger a fond memory. (Attention lawyers: we all know Mommy didn't pour this down junior's throat, any more than she tried to poison her wretched, ungrateful child.)

I hate Bosco
Bosco's bad for me.
Mommy put it in my milk
To try to poison me . . .
I fooled Mommy
I put it in her tea.
Now there is no Mommy
To try to poison me!

Lettered Revenge

If you are a music columnist fired from a New York daily in a purge ordered by a publisher more conscious of cost than quality, you write a particularly imaginative swansong column.

You take the publisher's name, but not in vain, for its letters just happen to be the anagram for a "new" rock group, say, Hurd Merc Troup. In your last column, you're obliged to report how knowledgeable critics agree that this gang has no talent whatsoever beyond how to make a buck by appealing to the basest human instincts.

Your column makes the first edition of your paper, and then a skeptical copy-editor gets out his Scrabble set . . .

Revenge of the News Nerds

Journalists at the underground newspaper, *eXile*, found their complaints about the *New York Times*' cozy coverage of Russian president Vladimir Putin and his government were being ignored, so the eXilers sought a striking way to get the gray old lady's attention. They burst into the Moscow offices of the Newspaper of Record and flung a pie into the face of bureau chief Michael Wines. Not just any kind of pie—but a truly disgusting pie—a horse-sperm pie.

Lest Wines not recognize its taste, prank perpetrator Mike Taibbi revealed the just desert's key ingredient to reporters of a rival New York paper. "You can't fight *The New York Times* with conventional weapons," explained Taibbi, who had taken the precaution of being photographed adding the secret ingredient before his creation met Wines' kisser.

Even in free Russia, obtaining equine sperm wasn't easy. Taibbi was able to pick up a vial of this special bodily fluid at a horse farm, only by convincing its manager that he was from a cosmetics company that needed the sperm for a new face cream. Taibbi had no regrets about inflicting this Godfather-inspired revenge on a fellow journalist. "He's an evil propagandist," Taibbi said.

Wines replied, "They can say whatever they want. My stories speak for themselves." Asked if he truly knew what hit him, Wines admitted, "Nothing would surprise me."

What's Playing in Hopkinton?

The Rev. Dennis James Robinson of Hopkinton, Massachusetts, has seen couples getting hitched with just about every hitch imaginable—including one very sweet couple who tied the knot in a 268-gallon Jacuzzi filled with 72 packages of Jell-O. Orange flavored.

But the most colorful wedding over which the Unitarian minister presided was a rather vengeful affair, he acknowledged in a newspaper interview.

As the ceremony was starting on a patio overlooking a golf course, he became vaguely aware that a ruckus was taking place somewhere behind him, but, being a professional, he ignored it.

Yet when it came time for the bride to say her vows, a breathy voice in back of him bellowed, "I do!"

The voice belonged to the groom's ex-girlfriend, outfitted in a wedding gown.

The groom turned to warn the wedding guests to be careful, as his former flame had recently broken into his house, trashed it and slit the tires on his car. Then, with the reverend's help, he hastily completed his marriage to the woman he intended to wed.

Meanwhile, after the chauffeur left the wedding couple's limousine for a moment, the angry ex attacked. She wrote "I Love You" on the hood of the vehicle in lighter fluid, then set the car aflame.

SWEETEST OF ALL

Ultimate Best revenge novel: *The Ax* by Donald Westlake

Ultimate Best revenge movie: *The Unforgiven*

Second ultimate Best revenge movie: *Tora! Tora! Tora!* (and its remake, *Pearl Harbor*)

UltimateBest revenge television program: *Judge Judy*

The Happy Hooker meets *How The West Was Won*: You can lead a whore to death but you can't make her friends shrink. William Munny (CLINT EASTWOOD) personifies revenge-for-hire in *The Unforgiven*.

Hollywood strikes back at Japan. in *Tora! Tora! Tora!* Some revenges are too good not to remake.

The Revenge Fizz

Get back at your hangover with this classic Ramos Gin Fizz.

2 ounces gin

2 ounces cream

1/2 ounce fresh lemon juice

1/2 ounce fresh lime juice

1 egg white

1 tablespoon powdered sugar

1 dash (3-4 drops) orange-flower water

Club soda on reserve

Pour all of the ingredients into a chilled cocktail mixer and shake furiously for at least one minute. Strain into a goblet and top off with cold club soda, to taste.

Alternate plan: Use a blender with about one quarter goblet of shaved ice. Then add soda and stir.

Warning: This libation will soothe one's nerves, which could render moot the very idea to seek revenge.

CHAPTER SIX

HAPPY

ENDINGS

One can't spend an entire life holding a grudge. One can't even spend an entire movie in a fit of pique. That's why Hollywood loves the "I-Hate-You-I-Can't-Live-Without-You" genre. You know the early signs: Friction when hero and heroine first meet. Followed by a heated exchange. Followed by a cooling down period. Followed by ardor.

Scenes We Wish We'd Lived

While it is nigh impossible to imagine FRED ASTAIRE and GINGER ROGERS in bed together (not that one couldn't have imagined her in bed with a lot of other guys—she did, after all, play "Anytime" Annie in *42nd Street*), it is impossible to imagine Ginger on the dance floor with anyone but Fred. Their formulaic RKO musicals invariably had them starting out as archenemies, as was the case in *Top Hat*. But by the final fadeout they are in each other's arms, where they belong.

RKO, 1935

WISECRACK ROMANCE

COLUMBIA, 1940

Ben Hecht and Charles MacArthur wrote the practically perfect play, *The Front Page*, but the Broadway smash did not become a battle of the sexes until clever movie director Howard Hawks took the story coed and cast CARY GRANT and ROSALIND RUSSELL to play, respectively, Walter Burns, the ruthless Chicago newspaper editor, and Hildy Johnson, crack reporter.

This sizzling remake, entitled *His Girl Friday*, also added the delightful tangent of Walter and Hildy having been recently divorced. Hildy's mistake is dropping in on Walter at the paper just as an innocent man is about to go to his death. She may hate Walter, but she loves a good story and, as it turns out, she really loves her ex, too.

Not the Playboy Type

Only KATHARINE HEPBURN could get away with playing a character named Bunny, which is something she did in one of the lesser but nonetheless charming *us* (as in women) vs. *them* (men) outings that pitted her against her real-life partner, SPENCER TRACY. In *Desk Set*, Tracy, under the perfectly acceptable name of Richard, plays a covert efficiency expert who arrives to computerize the TV-network library run by Bunny. In other words, he's seemingly there to see that she is replaced by a machine. The inevitable sparks fly but, by the end, so does some rice.

Like a Virgin

"This may come as a shock to you, but there are some men who don't end every sentence with a proposition!" Jan Morrow (DORIS DAY) to Brad Allen (ROCK HUDSON) in *Pillow Talk*. They end up on their way to see the preacher, of course.

UNIVERSAL, 1959

Charming Away Every Obstacle

Eve Kendell, as played by EVA MARIE SAINT, has every reason to hate Roger O. Thornhill (CARY GRANT) who may also be the spy George Kaplan in Alfred Hitchcock's *North By Northwest*. Our heroine, after all, is working for agents who are trying to trap and kill Kaplan. In this case, he really is the archenemy. But, of course, Thornhill's charm seduces her. Moviegoers, on the other hand, are seduced by Grant's being chased by a crop-duster and dangling off the end of Abraham Lincoln's nose. In the end, everyone we like wins.

MGM, 1959

SMELL AND SOUND

Spinster Marian, the librarian (SHIRLEY JONES), butts heads with traveling con man Harold Hill (ROBERT PRESTON), after he alights in River City, Iowa, to form a boys' band—and collect advance payment for its instruments. She smells a rat the minute she meets "the pro-fessor" and although she keeps picking up its scent, she holds her nose long enough to fall for his spell-binding, salesman ways. The movie, by the way, is *The Music Man*, the Valentine to Middle America when it sat squarely in the middle.

DINNER PARTIES THAT WON'T WORK

David Geffen	Britney Spears	Elton John
Michael Eisner	Christina Aguilera	Richard Simmons
Michael Ovitz	Jerry Lee Lewis	Brett Favre
Martha Stewart	Al Roker	
Jennifer Lopez	Bryant Gumbel	
Mike Tyson	Roger Ebert	

WOOF! WOOF!

No one said that archrivals have to be people. Dogs make perfectly suitable opponents, just as they make great friends. TOM HANKS stars as the small-town cop and compulsive neatnik, Scott Turner, in *Turner & Hooch*; the role of the drooling, destructive Hooch is played by a Dogue de Brodeaux. The beast makes a perfect hate object until he not only assists Turner in solving a murder case, but also teaches the bachelor how to love—in this case, a veterinarian.

THE END

SIN SERIES

Have you read...

VOLUME I

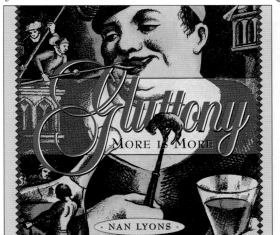

Volume II

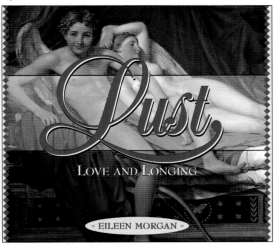

VOLUME III

VOLUME IV

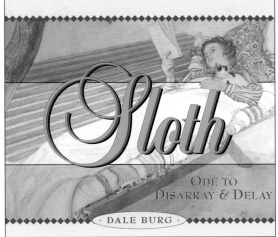

SIN SERIES

VOLUME VI

Coming soon...

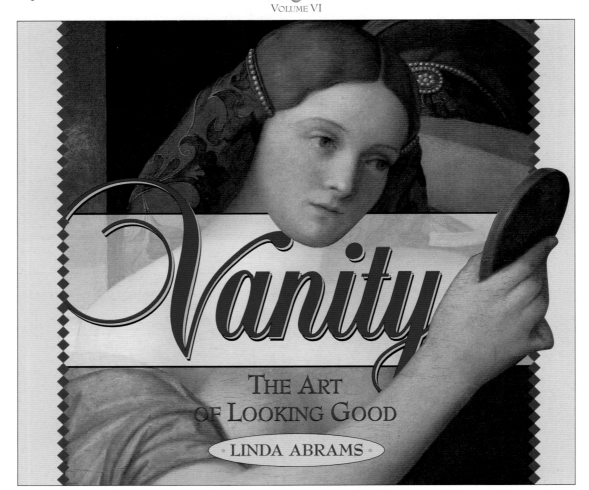

Vanity

THE ART
OF LOOKING GOOD

· LINDA ABRAMS ·

www.redrockpress.com